IN THE FOOTSTEPS OF [SHERLOCK HOLMES]

THE CASE OF THE MAN WHO FOLLOWED HIMSELF

A new Sherlock Holmes story based on the notebooks and papers of John H. Watson MD

Written and Researched by
ALLEN SHARP

Cambridge University Press
Cambridge
New York   Port Chester   Melbourne   Sydney

In the footsteps of Sherlock Holmes
The Case of the Baffled Policeman
The Case of the Buchanan Curse
The Case of the Devil's Hoofmarks
The Case of the Frightened Heiress
The Case of the Gentle Conspirators
The Case of the Howling Dog
The Case of the Man who Followed Himself
The Case of the Silent Canary

Published by the Press Syndicate of the University of Cambridge
The Pitt Building, Trumpington Street, Cambridge CB2 1RP
40 West 20th Street, New York, NY 10011, USA
10 Stamford Road, Oakleigh, Melbourne 3166, Australia

© Cambridge University Press 1990

First published 1990

Printed in Great Britain by the Guernsey Press Co. Ltd, Guernsey

British Library cataloguing in publication data
Sharp, Allen
The case of the man who followed himself – (Sharp, Allen. In the footsteps of Sherlock Holmes).
1. Title
823'.914[F]

ISBN 0 521 38956 9

The cover photograph is reproduced with permission from
City of Westminster: Sherlock Holmes Collection, Marylebone Library
The picture frame was loaned by Tobiass.
p.31 is reproduced by permission of Batsford.
pp.43 and 61 by Celia Hart   DS

About the Series

In 1881, Sherlock Holmes, while working in the chemical laboratory of St Bartholomew's hospital in London, met Dr John Watson, an army surgeon recently returned to England. Watson was looking for lodgings. Holmes had just found some which were too large for his needs, and wanted someone to share the rent. So it was that Holmes and Watson moved into 221B Baker Street. It was the beginning of a partnership which was to last more than twenty years and one which would make 221B Baker Street one of the most famous addresses in all of England.

Some credit for that partnership must also go to Mrs Hudson, Sherlock Holmes' landlady and housekeeper. It was she who put up with a lodger who made awful smells with his chemical experiments, who played the violin at any time of the day or night, who kept cigars in the coal scuttle, and who pinned his letters to the wooden mantlepiece with the blade of a knife!

So it is perhaps not unfitting that the only original documents which are known to have survived from those twenty years are now owned by Mrs Susan Stacey, a grandniece of that same Mrs Hudson. They include three of Dr Watson's notebooks or, more accurately, two notebooks and a diary which has been used as a notebook. The rest is an odd assortment, from letters and newspaper clippings to photographs and picture postcards. The whole collection has never been seen as anything more than a curiosity. The notebooks do not contain any complete accounts of cases – only jottings – though some of these were very probably made on the spot in the course of actual investigations. Occasionally, something has been pinned or pasted to a page of a notebook. There are some rough sketches and, perhaps the most interesting, there are many ideas and questions which Watson must have noted down so that he could discuss them with Holmes at some later time.

But now, by using Watson's notebooks, old newspaper reports, police files, and other scraps of information which the documents provide, it has been possible to piece together some of Holmes' cases which have never before been published. In each story, actual pages from the notebooks, or other original documents, have been included. They will be found in places where they add some information, provide some illustration, or pick out what may prove to be important clues.

But it is hoped that they also offer something more. By using your imagination, these pages can give **you** the opportunity to relive the challenge, the excitement and, occasionally, the danger which Watson, who tells the stories, must himself have experienced in working with Sherlock Holmes – the man so often described as "the world's greatest detective".

Chapter One

A Haunting Likeness

~~~

I had very recently purchased the first issue of a new threepenny monthly, *Harmsworth's Magazine*. It was a not unfamiliar mixture of short stories and various items of a general interest. The first article was entitled, "Notable Doubles in Real Life" and was most generously illustrated with photographic evidence. Some of the instances given, I did already know – like the quite remarkable resemblance between the Czar of Russia and the Duke of York. Most I did not know, an example being the likeness between the famous statesman, Cecil Rhodes and Sir John Stainer, professor of music at Oxford.

Though Sherlock Holmes had always shown an undisguised contempt for most of my reading material, this was one of the very few occasions where I had felt the subject to be of sufficient interest to draw the article to his attention. Not

The Case of the Man who Followed Himself

entirely unexpectedly, his reaction to it had been politely dismissive and the subject was one which I had promptly forgotten. It was certainly not a matter in my mind on that hot July afternoon when, having just finished a late lunch, we had an unexpected visitor. It was a young man, who had given his name as Baroncourt. According to Mrs Hudson, he was not only insisting that his seeing Sherlock Holmes was a matter of life and death, but his appearance and demeanour suggested that he, at least, believed it to be the truth.

Over the years, the doorstep of 221B Baker Street had been the scene of so many similarly dramatic entreaties, though so few of any worth, that Holmes showed a predictable reluctance to see the visitor. The fact that he did, in the end, agree was probably more out of consideration for Mrs Hudson's plainly stated concern for the state of her dough, rapidly rising in a hot kitchen, than out of any regard for whatever was troubling the distressed youth waiting on the doorstep!

Julius Baroncourt was a young man whom I would have placed in his mid-twenties, though he had a much greater air of maturity and self-confidence than I would expect of most men of his age. It suggested to me that he came of good stock and had, most probably, enjoyed the advantages of an education at one of the better public schools. Other than that he was sweating rather freely, he was unremarkable in appearance, of medium height, hair mid-brown, fresh faced, and clean

A Haunting Likeness

A photograph from the article, "Notable Doubles in Real Life", which appeared in the first issue of Harmsworth's Magazine, *published in July 1898.*

W. & D. Downey, photo, Ebury Street.
H.I.M. THE CZAR AND H.R.H. THE DUKE OF YORK.

The Case of the Man who Followed Himself

shaven. He was both neatly and soberly dressed, in clothes of good quality, but looking to have done good service. I placed him either among the genteel poor or as one who had fallen upon hard times. That Holmes would already have deduced much more was soon to be confirmed.

"Watson," he said, "though I know it is you who would normally do any prescribing, can I suggest that this young man is in considerable need of a long, cold drink. Having suffered some unpleasant experience in the reading room of the British Museum, having walked there from St James's Park and then to Baker Street, he is distressed both by his experience and the heat. The latter might be the more easily remedied. I see that there is still standing on the table an unused glass and a half jug of Mrs Hudson's excellent lemonade."

In following Holmes' suggestion, I missed the expression on young Baroncourt's face. But I could guess what it was as I heard Holmes going on to explain what, to the uninitiated, must always have sounded like a demonstration of psychic powers!

"A simple matter of observation and deduction," he had begun. "The piece of paper which you have twice smoothed out since you entered the room, and which you are again nervously crushing in your right hand, I recognise as the slip which you are required to fill out in the British Museum library, stating your book requirements.

Since it has writing upon it, and since you still have it, I take it that something occurred at about that time, causing you to leave the library without fulfilling your original purpose in going there.

"You have not removed all traces of bread crumbs from your clothes, their presence suggesting that you have lunched out of doors. Two of those crumbs are lodged in the toe of one of your shoes – an unusual place for them to be unless you were throwing the bread, I would imagine, in the act of feeding ducks. Most other London birds, such as pigeons, would have had the boldness to remove them, even from your shoe. I choose St James's Park merely as being more likely than either Hyde or Regent's Park. Your heated and, when you entered, slightly breathless state is enough to tell me that you walked from the British Museum – though you felt your journey here was pressing. It follows that it is even less likely that you took a cab from the park to the museum."

Holmes was, as ever, completely correct, though I would have thought that his picking upon St James's Park was something of a lucky guess! There was no doubt that his habit of treating a newly arrived visitor to some dazzling display of his deductive powers was often done for no other reason than that he enjoyed doing it. But it did serve other purposes – a fact of which he was undoubtedly aware. Not least, it had a noticeably calming effect upon the most nervous of clients – perhaps suddenly convinced that if any-

The Case of the Man who Followed Himself

one were to solve their problem, who more likely than a man of such clearly remarkable abilities! It worked with Baroncourt. He had stopped crushing the piece of paper and held his glass in a now steady hand when he answered Holmes' eventual question of what it was that had brought him to Baker Street.

"I have a double, Mr Holmes."

"How extraordinary!" I exclaimed.

"My colleague," Holmes said, "is not referring to the fact of your having a double, but rather to the coincidence that he has, within these last few days, drawn my attention to a magazine article upon that very subject. It was, I fear, in keeping with the standard of work one expects of such popular publications – very superficial. It dealt with none of the more interesting aspects, like how it is possible to create an apparent similarity in the appearance of two quite dissimilar faces, merely by reshaping the cutting of the facial hair. But I digress, Mr Baroncourt. You did not come here merely to tell me that you have a double."

Baroncourt gave no immediate answer.

Sensing that the young man was perhaps having some difficulty in finding the appropriate words, I suggested the most common circumstance in which the possession of a double can prove to be a matter for concern. "Is it," I asked, "a case of deliberate impersonation?"

This time, the response *was* immediate.

"No, Dr Watson, it is nothing like that. My difficulty is in explaining it in a manner that will not give you cause to question my sanity. Yet if I had to define it in a few words, I should have to say that it is as if I were being haunted by him!"

Holmes, who I suspected had until this moment supposed that he was dealing with no more than an over-anxious young man, displayed a sudden alertness of manner, recognisable at least to myself, as a first sign of genuine interest.

"Many strange stories have been told within these walls," he said. "Few have proved to be any reflection upon the sanity of the teller. You say that you have a double. You might best begin by explaining the circumstances in which you first became aware of it."

"It was not a sudden discovery," Baroncourt answered. "It was, rather, a matter of slow realisation, over a period of what must have been many weeks. It began with nothing more than the casual and apparently innocent remark of some acquaintance. Because I did not then attach any importance to it, I cannot recall the exact words of the first instance. But let us say that it was, 'I saw you this morning in Kensington High Street'. I knew that to have been impossible, simply because I was in some totally different place at that time."

"It's happened to me," I said, "more than once. It's a classic case of mistaken identity, often based upon a quite fleeting glimpse of someone who, in truth, bears little real resemblance to oneself."

The Case of the Man who Followed Himself

"I do realise that, Dr Watson. Even when these false sightings of myself began to occur with great frequency, I still didn't treat them as a matter for concern. Indeed, I do remember making a joke about having a double, expressing the hope that it was not someone whose habits might be such as to bring my own into any kind of disrepute!"

"But clearly, that unconcerned attitude has now changed," Holmes interjected. "What has happened to change it?"

Again I sensed that there was some hesitancy in Baroncourt's reply.

"I would not wish it to sound flippant, Mr Holmes, but, quite simply, you might say that my double moved in off the streets. He began to frequent those very same establishments which I did myself, including my club!"

"Which is?" Holmes asked.

"Boul's" was the answer. It is one of the less expensive, though none the less respectable of the many gentlemen's clubs in the vicinity of St James's Square.

"Then," Holmes continued. "you do at least know who this person – this double – is."

"No, Mr Holmes. I do not."

....

Frequently, I did not instantly follow Holmes' reasoning. But, on this occasion, I was sure that I did. If Baroncourt's double had begun to frequent the same club, it would seem impossible that he did not know who he was. London clubs – and

Boul's would be no exception – were not establishments into which one could simply walk, without the near certainty of being challenged, if one were not a member. Entrance halls were invariably manned by those chosen, it would seem, for their eagle eye and impeccable memory. Every member would be recognised upon sight and known by name and title. Non-members would be admitted only if they were accompanied by a member and would be required to sign the visitor's book. If Baroncourt's double *were* a member then both his name and his remarkable resemblance to another member would be known. If he were not a member, then his name would have to appear in the visitor's book.

"No, Mr Holmes," Baroncourt repeated, "and for a simple reason. My double is, apparently, so exactly identical in appearance to myself, that he is taken to be myself, and is therefore admitted without question."

"So you do not know the name of your double. You have just said, 'apparently' identical. Do I take it that you have not seen him?"

"I have not."

"Then tell me. Do you visit your club on regular days, and at regular times of the day? Are your visits, in other words, in any degree predictable?"

"No – other than that I call at some time upon most days to collect letters. Some of my business is done through correspondence and I frequently use the club as my business address."

The Case of the Man who Followed Himself

"And upon those occasions when it came to your knowledge that your club had been visited by your double, did you learn anything of what he might have been doing there?"

"To my knowledge, Mr Holmes, it would appear that he has done nothing." Baroncourt paused. "I know that it sounds strange, but it is almost the literal truth. He was seen in the club. It seems that he has spoken to no-one. I cannot discover that he has ever partaken of either food or drink. He has signed for nothing on my account."

"You said that he had begun to frequent 'places' which you yourself –"

Baroncourt interrupted.

"Perhaps, Mr Holmes, I can save you some time. I would have to tell you much the same story of all the places which I know him to have visited. If, as I imagine, you are seeking to establish some motive for this man's behaviour, there is none of which I know or might even guess. I only wish to God that there were! The man has never besmirched either my name or character. He has never made any gain from me, either financial or in kind. Indeed, if such *were* his motive, then he would have made a poor choice of victim!"

Holmes might well have pursued this line of questioning, but it was Baroncourt who chose that moment to relate something to us of his personal circumstances. He had, he said, only one living relative, an uncle, Silas Baroncourt, who owned Selsdon Park, a sizeable estate some

A Haunting Likeness

25 miles west of London, and 8 miles north of the main Oxford road. Julius Baroncourt visited his uncle regularly, usually upon a Sunday.

"There is," he said, "little affection between my uncle and myself. Perhaps a part of the fault is mine. I've always found it difficult to form any close human relationship. I've had few friends in my life and am, by nature, a solitary person – often moody and ill-tempered, I'm told. What is certain is that I find no pleasure in my visits to Selsdon Park, and I see none for my uncle, though it is he who insists upon them. As the sole heir to his fortune he sees me as having an obligation to accede to his wishes, though I've often questioned the worth of it to me.

"My uncle Silas is a man still in his sixties, and enjoys the rudest of health. He might even outlive me! Such benefits as I now enjoy from what he describes as his 'charity', are modest indeed. He is the most miserly of individuals, even towards himself. In that huge house he has no full-time servants – only a man, and I think, two women from the village of Selsdon who come upon certain days, but never upon a Sunday. Whatever there is to eat in the house on the occasions of my visits, it is never anything other than cold food. The servants see only to such things as my uncle considers to be essential. And cleanliness is not among them! As to myself, he makes me an allowance which does little more than pay for a miserable lodging – a single, third storey room in

The Case of the Man who Followed Himself

a much dilapidated house in the Edgware Road. I need to afford my club, so that I can at least do business from a respectable address."

I asked Baroncourt what was his business.

"Somewhat uncertain!" was the reply. "I buy and sell – rare books, letters, manuscripts – whatever I feel I might turn to some profit. Some items I sell to dealers in the city. I have a few private customers. I always need some modest capital to do business at all, but my funds at any one time are highly unpredictable. In truth, Mr Holmes, it has crossed my mind, that I may well not be able to afford this present conversation!"

"You are obviously an intelligent man. If for the reason you have just suggested you have not previously sought any professional help in this singular affair, you must surely have, yourself, attempted to resolve the mystery."

....

It transpired that Baroncourt *had* sought some professional help though, not unexpectedly, his first action had been to attempt to enquire further of those who had reported to him the numerous appearances of his double. He had not, he said, accounted for the manner in which such enquiries might be received. When those appearances had been confined to some fleeting glimpse in the street, the idea of Baroncourt having a double was readily accepted. What he had not anticipated was that once his double had, in his own words, "moved in off the streets" and begun to frequent such places as his club, attitudes would suddenly change.

"Though it was not said in as many words, Mr Holmes, the reactions were unmistakable. Either it was seen as a source of embarrassment, for which I was somehow held responsible, or it raised questions as to my sanity. I very soon felt that I simply could not pursue such enquiries."

He'd then gone to the police – but only to be told that as no crime had been committed, there was nothing they could do to help him. He had next tried a private enquiry agency, *Oldroyd and Hughes* in The Strand.

"I have been sent the occasional client by them," Holmes told him, "though not of recent years. But I would suppose them still to be reasonably capable and thorough in their investigations – as such agencies go."

"I did form that impression," Baroncourt agreed, "though they did prove to be of very little practical assistance. In fairness to the agency, I would have to say that it is possible that they could have done more. It was I who found myself unable to continue to afford to pay them what was, for me, a very considerable fee."

Holmes had been filling his pipe. Without looking up from that task, he asked, "And was it they who suggested you change your appearance?"

"No, Mr Holmes. The idea was . . ."

Holmes raised his eyes in response to the sudden hesitation. He commented:

The Case of the Man who Followed Himself

"A simple observation, of no importance in itself. I merely noted that you had recently removed your moustache. A slight reddening of the skin on your upper lip, not seen elsewhere on your face, tells me that it is still sensitive to the unfamiliar attentions of the razor."

"Your observation is correct. I was about to say that the idea was my own. I had thought . . ."

"Yes, yes!" Holmes exclaimed, I thought a little impatiently, "I do see your reasons. I am much more interested to know why the idea failed. Your presence here is ample evidence of that failure."

Baroncourt once again showed some hesitancy.

"I did tell you, Mr Holmes, that I might have difficulty in telling my story in a manner which would not cause you to doubt my sanity. The attempt to change my appearance did fail. It failed because my double had apparently removed his own moustache within hours of my removing mine – and in circumstances where no-one, I repeat 'no-one' but myself, could have known what I had done!"

"I see," Holmes said. "I see that you must have found that discovery not merely remarkable, but I should have thought quite disturbing – though neither remarkable nor disturbing enough to have brought you here. Had that discovery been the event which you experienced today in the British Museum, you would have given your account of it in quite different terms."

Baroncourt was clearly going to reply, but

A Haunting Likeness

Holmes had held up his hand in a gesture which conveyed his own desire to continue.

"You are going to tell me of that event, Mr Baroncourt. In a moment, you shall. But explain to me first, one thing which considerably puzzles me. You expressed some confidence in the abilities of Oldroyd and Hughes. You said that you left them because you could no longer afford their fees. Yet you come to me, knowing – as your earlier remarks suggested, that my services might prove to be still more expensive!".

Baroncourt was silent for some moments.

"I also said, Mr Holmes, that I have to retain a modest capital in order to carry out my business. If it costs me that capital to retain my sanity, I'd consider it money well spent. I told you truthfully, I believe Oldroyd and Hughes to have done their best to serve me well, yet I cannot rid myself of the feeling that they were relieved when I dispensed with their services. I will not say that they thought me mad, but I could not blame them for supposing that much of what I had told them was no more than fantasy. Were I to go back to them now, they would surely be convinced of it.

"I've told the circumstances of my failure in changing my appearance. Today, Mr Holmes, as you rightly deduced, I'd taken a light alfresco lunch in St James's Park. You already know the nature of my business. Some unusual manuscripts have recently come into my hands, the historical origins of which are uncertain. I had decided, while eating my lunch, to research the matter in the reading room of the British Museum – a place I do use, though infrequently. As I entered the museum library, the attendant on duty, a man with whom I do have slight acquaintance, said to me, 'Back again Mr Baroncourt. I gather you didn't find what you were wanting this morning.' You might think that something which, in my circumstances, could not have surprised me. It did not do so for several minutes, not until I was filling in the request form for the books that I required. It was not that my double had been to the same place as myself. It was a sudden realisation that on each occasion, other than those early sightings upon the streets, my double was *always* there before me. And, as upon this occasion, in places where he had been *before* my intention to visit that same spot had even been in my own mind."

For the first time since the very beginning of that long interview, Baroncourt, once more, looked less than composed.

"Mr Holmes, this man does not only look like me, he can read my thoughts, even before they have come into my conscious mind. He does not follow *me*. It is as if, unknowingly, it is *I* who follow him! I have never seen him. I do not know his name. He does nothing to me – takes nothing from me. In Heaven's name, what does he want? Who is he? Mr Holmes, you have got to help me before I do indeed lose my sanity!"

Chapter Two

Things Best Left Be

The private enquiry agency of Oldroyd and Hughes has its offices at 399B The Strand, occupying the third floor and attics of the same building as Romano's. Romano's, a restaurant opened in 1885 by a waiter from the Café Royal, had in the space of only a few years achieved a considerable reputation as a fashionable eating place – one to which I had, for some long time, promised myself a visit.

Holmes, having arranged an appointment at the agency for two that afternoon, I saw it as an obvious opportunity to have lunch at Romano's. Knowing Holmes' total lack of adventurousness in food, I should have been prepared for his counter suggestion that we eat instead at Simpson's where, as he truthfully said, the service was quick, the beef and mutton always reliable, and the charges modest. His added offer

The Case of the Man who Followed Himself

to pay for it would have made any argument on my part sound ungracious.

Simpson's Tavern, having long enjoyed popularity amongst the City's businessmen as a lunch-time venue, it was expectedly, quite crowded – though being a Saturday, with some establishments closed in the afternoon, not impossibly so. I had pointed out a table by the door, about to be vacated, and was therefore surprised to find Holmes pushing his way to the farther end of the room, to another table which was already occupied, admittedly by only one man. The man was, it seemed, too preoccupied with his eating to notice our arrival, looking up only when – again to my surprise – Holmes addressed him.

"May I introduce my colleague, Dr John Watson. Watson, this is my old friend and mentor, Ex-Chief Inspector Jack Oldroyd of Scotland Yard."

The Ex-Chief Inspector was clearly a man of both considerable age and girth. The combination presented him with some obvious difficulty in his attempt to rise from the cramped space between seat and table – an attempt that he wisely abandoned, eventually extending a podgy hand towards me from a reseated position.

"Mr Oldroyd of 'Oldroyd and Hughes'?" I enquired.

"You might say, 'as were'," the man answered, "more than 'as is'."

Holmes had now seated himself at the table and motioned me to do the same.

Things Best Left Be

"You've retired altogether from the business?" he asked.

"Half," Oldroyd replied. "That or thereabouts – the weather, flat feet, the veins, the tubes, and other such policeman's ailments permitting." The breathless and wheezing manner in which he spoke identified to which "tubes" he was referring. He looked at his plate – near overflowing with roast beef, Yorkshire puddings, potatoes and cabbage – and then at me. "And if you're thinking, Doctor Watson, that they're all ailments that might be a sight better for me losing a bit of weight, then I'll be telling you that I've got every intention of continuing to enjoy doing what may very likely be killing me!"

"What he's not telling you, Watson," Holmes said, "is that the point's becoming a bit academic. How old is it – eighty-two, or is it eighty-three?"

"Eighty-four, come August, Mr Holmes – and best not reminded of it."

Holmes had said, only yesterday during that memorable interview with Julius Baroncourt, that he'd had clients from the firm of Oldroyd and Hughes. His added rider, "not of recent years", I had taken as meaning that that was in the very earliest days of our sharing the rooms at Baker Street. At that time, Holmes still had few clients who approached him directly for assistance. He relied rather upon a mutual arrangement with a number of agencies – like Oldroyd and Hughes. In return for Holmes' giving them advice, they

The Case of the Man who Followed Himself

would send him clients with whom, for some reason, they preferred not to deal themselves. From my still quite vivid recollections of the strange, not to say sometimes sinister appearance of the callers at 221B in those days, I suspect the reason most often to have been that the agencies saw them as not sufficiently profitable.

It was also the basis of a long-standing joke between Holmes and myself. Holmes had not then thought to tell me the nature of his profession. I had not thought to ask. And the sudden appearance of this most motley collection of callers convinced me that it were better not to ask – I was already certain that Sherlock Holmes' occupation, if not actually criminal, was at the very least unsavoury!

But I stray from my point. The conversation between Holmes and Oldroyd suggested a closeness of relationship that could hardly have sprung from the circumstances which I describe. The mystery was soon resolved. Early in the ensuing conversation, it transpired that if Sherlock Holmes could ever be said to have had a schoolboy hero, Ex-Chief Inspector Jack Oldroyd was he.

....

Born in 1814, the young Oldroyd had been one of the last of the famous "Bow Street Runners". As Sergeant Oldroyd, he was one of the fifteen men who, until 1869, formed the whole of the then "Detective Branch". In 1860, he'd accompanied

Things Best Left Be

Detective Inspector Whicher to assist the Wiltshire police in the investigation of the notorious Road-Hill House Murder. Their remarkable work in that case has led to continuing speculation as to whether it was Whicher or Oldroyd upon whom Mr Wilkie Collins based his redoubtable "Sergeant Cuff" of *The Moonstone*.

By 1868, Oldroyd had himself been promoted to Detective Inspector and it was in that year that Sherlock Holmes, then a fourteen year old schoolboy at Winchester College, had first begun to read in the newspapers of Oldroyd's remarkable successes in the detection of crime. Oldroyd was certainly one reason for Holmes' first interest in detection. The two of them had eventually become acquainted during Holmes' time at Oxford and it was Oldroyd, himself about to retire from the police and set up in business as a private agency, who has most helped and encouraged Holmes in his ambition to become the world's first consulting detective.

It was therefore understandable that so much of our time lunching together should be taken up with reminiscences of times past. Yet one thing did puzzle me – there had been no mention of the business that had actually brought us to The Strand. My understanding was that the man with whom we were eating was the same man with whom we had an appointment at two o'clock. It was a mystery only deepened by Oldroyd's suddenly asking whether it was anything specific

The Case of the Man who Followed Himself

which had brought us to Simpson's that day! My natural response – that I had thought that *he* was – brought only smiles to the faces of my two companions.

"Ah! Watson," Holmes said, "my earlier enquiry of Mr Oldroyd as to whether he had now retired, should have told you that it was not he. Our appointment is with Oldroyd and Hughes, but the Mr Oldroyd who we are to see is Lawrence and not Jack."

"And what is it," Oldroyd asked, "that you are hoping my son can do for you?"

"No more than confirm some facts given to me by a client who recently employed your agency. I do so with that client's permission."

"And a client to whom *we* very obviously failed to give satisfaction," Oldroyd observed. "As you can see, Holmes, my days of tramping the streets are over, but I use the little time I spend in the office to keep a finger on most of what's going on. What's your client's name?"

Holmes told him. Oldroyd's only immediate reaction was to grab the arm of a passing waiter, expressing the desire to have his tankard recharged with ale and to follow his main course with a "good helping" of Syrup Roly-Poly. It was not until he had some of the latter in his mouth that he made any attempt to resume the conversation – though at first this seemed to be in no way related to anything which had gone before.

"You know that I'm a Yorkshireman?"

"You do retain a trace of that accent," Holmes answered. It was a teasing understatement, but one that was ignored.

"Scarborough's where I was born," Oldroyd continued, "born and raised. There's a church in Scarborough, name of St Mary's. And there's a tale told that if you was to stand in the church porch just afore each midnight on the Eve of St Mark, then come the third year you'd see them who was about to die, pass into the church. Not the real folk, understand. *You* might call them 'doubles'. In Yorkshire, we calls them 'wafts'.

"When I were still a lad, there were one of those I goes about with, name of Fred Ormesby – madder than most, but good company. Fred did tell us that he'd started to keep watch in the porch of St Mary's church, though I'd doubt that any of us believed him, no more than we did when he said that he'd been for the third year, and seen the wafts. Maybe because we didn't believe him he wouldn't tell us no more. And he never did, it being less than a month after that Fred Ormesby was drowned in Scarborough harbour.

"But that wasn't an end to it. It seems as Fred *had* told his mother what he saw – and it was after Fred's funeral that she told my mother. He hadn't recognised nobody as he'd seen going into the church – except one. That one were himself."

Oldroyd had started to spoon the syrup from the plate and carefully distribute it over what remained of the suet pastry. I could see the obvi-

The Case of the Man who Followed Himself

ous connection between Oldroyd's story and that which Baroncourt had related to us on the previous afternoon – though the connection was, to say the least, remote. A piece of Yorkshire folklore, and what some unfortunate child imagined he'd seen at midnight in some dark and, doubtless, ghostly churchyard, surely had little bearing upon Baroncourt's double – who had been witnessed by many and in broad daylight. I waited for Holmes to give some lead, but he did not. It was Oldroyd who went on.

"I tell you that story because I know it to be true – so far as anybody can know the truth of such a tale. I could have told you others that I knew from folk who'd no reason to lie. There's wafts been seen at times and places where them as saw them had no cause to think they weren't real, not that is till they spoke about it to the one who was real and were told that *they'd* been nowhere near the place where the waft was seen. And if it happened, then you could be sure that the real person would be dead within the year."

If Oldroyd's addition to his original story had made the connection with Baroncourt a deal clearer, it had equally added to my confusion of mind. I was now wondering whether Oldroyd was joking or whether, despite the man's impressive professional record, he was showing earlier symptoms of senility! Perhaps it was because of some visible sign of my embarrassment that Oldroyd was prompted to add, "Believe it, Doctor

Watson. Wafts can look as real as you or I. There could be one sitting at that table opposite – and you might not know it."

Involuntarily, I turned my head.

"Not to worry, Doctor. Wafts never speak. All of them's been talking – I think. At any road, none of them I'd say looks exactly like you!"

Holmes had started to laugh, loudly.

"He's been joking!" I said, not without some sense of relief.

"He was joking," Holmes answered, "but not, I suspect, in drawing a most interesting parallel between the Baroncourt affair and a very ancient superstition. I'd remind you, Watson, that the story Baroncourt told us certainly appears to be a mystery, but only if one assumes his story is true. All that my friend Oldroyd is telling us is that he is satisfied that it is true."

"Satisfied enough," was Oldroyd's reply. "Enough to decide that that was one client I'd be happier to be rid of." He raised his spoon in a gesture which seemed to convey that he hadn't finished what he wanted to say. "I know you'd not think that a proper answer, and I'd not be sure that I can give you one that is. No doubt the man told you that he didn't engage our services for too long – but long enough for us to turn up a few facts that didn't sit comfortable in my mind, and to bring back things I'd thought long forgotten. Bad dreams. I was back on Scarborough harbour when they pulled Fred's body out of the water. I

The Case of the Man who Followed Himself

saw the funeral again, heard my mother tell me what Fred had seen at the church, and what she said to me after it – 'Learn your lesson, Jack. Always remember that some things in this world are best left be'." His spoon rattled down onto the empty plate. Then, with a sudden briskness, he said, "When you go to the office, tell Lawrie that you've seen me and that I said to give you all the notes we gave to Baroncourt – as well as the one's that we didn't. I'll not tell you to make up your own mind, Holmes – 'cause I know you will."

"One question," I said. "You implied that you got rid of Baroncourt. He told us that he dispensed with your services because he could no longer afford them."

"He would," was the answer. "I saw to it that he was told what it would cost him for us to continue. It would very likely have given Croesus a sleepless night!"

Oldroyd did not accompany us to the office. It was, he said, too hot, too far and too soon – for an old man's digestion. As we left Simpson's, I asked Holmes what he had made of the conversation.

"What should I make of it?" he answered. "I'd have thought it all too obvious. Oldroyd finds that he's got a client who's having trouble with a waft. And he told you what that means – that the man would be dead within the year. Clearly he needed to be rid of him in case Baroncourt should die without paying his fee. Remember, Watson, Oldroyd is a Yorkshireman!"

Things Best Left Be

Simpson's Tavern in The Strand.

Chapter Three

A Second Helping

It must be said of Sherlock Holmes that at those times when he had determined not to be forthcoming he did show variety in his methods of achieving it. It might be total mental withdrawal. It might be a simple avoidance of answering questions – whether by a blunt refusal to do so, or the irritatingly unsubtle device of suddenly changing the topic of conversation. Such flippancy as he'd displayed on our leaving Simpson's, was yet another. It was the one that I liked least, being always left with the feeling that it might have contained some grain of truth – which I had, invariably, missed!

Perhaps in this particular instance it was of little account. The Strand was so crowded and noisy that it was near impossible to stay together on the pavement, much less to continue with any kind of conversation. We at last completed a bruising passage to 399B and ascended the six flights of narrow, uncarpeted stairs to the office of Oldroyd and Hughes.

Hughes, Oldroyd's original partner who had followed a similar if less spectacular career in the Metropolitan Police, had died some five years earlier. The business was, effectively, run by Lawrence Oldroyd, with the assistance of what his father had described as "some youngsters" – the youngest of whom was forty-one! I had hoped that, in the absence of any ready assistance from Holmes, Lawrence Oldroyd might shed new light upon what I still regarded as his father's bizarre theory. But it was not to be. Lawrence was as taciturn as his father was voluble, saying little more than was necessary to accomplish the handing over of the records of the Baroncourt investigation.

We returned, therefore, quite quickly to the crowded street, its unpleasantness made no less so by a temperature which felt unusually high and humid, even for a fine July day in London. I welcomed Holmes' suggestion that we find a cab, rather than attempt our return journey to Baker Street on foot. The cabs, it seemed, were as full as were the pavements. The omnibuses offered no better alternative, pairs of sweating horses straining to haul vehicles, not merely full within and on top, but with determined passengers clinging steadfastly to the outside in a manner reminiscent of flies stuck on a strip of treacled paper!

The Case of the Man who Followed Himself

We were no very great distance from Charing Cross Station, from which we could have travelled by way of the underground railway to Baker Street Station. But it was not a suggestion that I sought to make. Holmes had a number of oft expressed dislikes which included telephones, electric lighting, horseless carriages – and underground railways. That last, I shared with him. With the carriage windows open there was an uninterrupted flow of sulphurous fumes from the engine. With the windows closed the carriages were rapidly filled with the equally noxious fumes of ill-burning oil lamps. The underground railway perhaps offered less to alternative forms of transport than it did to methods of asphyxiation!

I had, therefore, resigned myself to the lesser discomfort of walking, when a cab drew up almost alongside us, its passenger hailing us by name. It was Chief Inspector Alec Macdonald, of whose recent promotion I'd heard, but whom neither Holmes nor I had seen for some years. Upon hearing of our difficulty in obtaining a cab, he suggested that we share his. He was returning to Scotland Yard – a little out of our way, but if we were willing to accompany him that far, we could then use the cab to return us to Baker Street. It was an offer readily accepted.

Having dropped Macdonald, and seeking to avoid the worst of the traffic, our cabby took us from Charing Cross to the west end of Piccadilly by way of the quieter streets, including York

A Second Helping

Street, in which Boul's Club is situated. Having acquired an interest in that establishment, it was natural that I should pay particular attention to the building as we passed by. What I had not expected was to see none other than Baroncourt himself, just entering it. By the time I could draw Holmes' attention to the fact, Baroncourt was gone.

"Yesterday," I said, "Baroncourt told us that he was returning immediately to Hadleigh in Suffolk, where he had acquired the manuscripts to which he referred, and where he was hoping to complete some financial transaction. I should have thought that 'immediately' would mean this morning at the latest."

"I fear," Holmes answered, "that 'immediately' is a word not always used in its literal sense. He could still be returning today, and I see nothing that we can, or indeed should, do about it. You will recall that he agreed to any enquiries being made, except at two places, his uncle's home at Selsdon Park, and his club. And he did, it would seem, have adequate reasons for both of those exclusions."

....

The windows of our living room at 221B Baker Street faced east. In consequence, even at the height of the summer, the room had usually lost the sun by late morning, affording a welcome relief from the heat of days such as this. Despite the always tepid temperature of London tap-

35

water, Mrs Hudson – with, she had assured us, the aid of nothing more than covers of wet muslin – contrived to produce a surprisingly cool and refreshing lemonade. It was after consuming two glasses, and now using a finger idly to stir the slices of lemon that remained at the bottom of the empty jug, that Holmes remarked, "I take it, Watson, that you would not subscribe to Oldroyd's theory that Baroncourt's double is a waft."

I thought that question hardly necessary. I'd no doubt that Oldroyd had been an outstanding policeman – in his time. I felt equally certain that age had begun to tell on him – not altogether surprisingly, at eighty-four. "I admit," I said, "that he tells a story well. Though I feel foolish about it now, I believe that he even succeeded in having *me* worried for a moment. But the fact remains, Holmes, that what he was recounting was nothing more than some piece of local superstitious nonsense. I did think that you dealt with it very tactfully."

Holmes removed his finger from the jug.

"I was not attempting to be tactful. You see, Watson. I think that you may have misjudged a number of things – one most certainly. The belief in wafts is one of the most ancient and universal of superstitions, albeit that the waft is known by many other names.

"In these islands, you may hear it called a 'fetch', or a 'wraith'. Brewer, in his most excellent work on phrase and fable, calls it a 'double-walker'. The Greeks and Romans had several words for it. It is the *'fylgjar'* of the Norsemen. The Germans call it a *'doppelgänger'*. Nor are such beliefs confined to the ignorant. I recall that the composer, Glück, recorded such a personal encounter."

"You aren't telling me that you believe in such things."

"No, Watson – merely explaining my response to Oldroyd's stories. I said they provide an interesting parallel with Baroncourt's account of his double. As Oldroyd truthfully told you, wafts are reputed never to speak. Baroncourt said the same of his double. Wafts usually appear in places where the real person is not. In Baroncourt's case, not only does he claim that to be true, but suggests something still more remarkable. His double appears with apparent regularity, in places which he himself frequents at completely unpredictable times. Yet the double never appears at the same time as himself! And most strange of all. Baroncourt's double appears, it seems, 'before him'. In the Norse tradition, the double, or *fylgjar* was said frequently to precede the real person – so that, it was believed, the spirit double might thereby see into the future."

I still didn't see the point that Holmes was making.

"That, Watson, may well be because I haven't yet made it! I'm suggesting only that I feel your judgement of Oldroyd to be hasty. Age has,

The Case of the Man who Followed Himself

doubtless taken its toll. I'd suspect the man to be indulging in what are euphemistically called, 'the privileges of old age' – in truth, a less than critical assessment of evidence, allowing emotion and sentiment to cloud the judgement. Age, Watson, brings with it, frequent thoughts of death. It is not unnatural that the old are more ready to accept what might appear to be evidence of the supernatural, of life after death. I have yet to examine the records that we have brought with us from his office. Yet I will predict with complete confidence that they hold a few surprises – more than sufficient, I suspect Watson, to cause you to re-assess some of your present conclusions. Age may have blunted the sharpness of his reasoning. Ex-Chief Inspector Jack Oldroyd may be mistaken, but he is a long way from being senile."

....

I confess to being one of those readers of mystery stories who, having become bored with the plot, or even particularly excited by it, can rarely resist the temptation to turn to the last page to seek the solution of the mystery. I know full well that it will serve only to destroy what pleasure I might have derived had I continued in my reading, and this knowledge has taught me, in my own recording of Sherlock Holmes' cases, never to place the whole solution in that position.

The amount of paper we had brought with us from The Strand was considerably more than I had expected and clearly demanded several hours

A Second Helping

of careful study to do justice to it. Oldroyd had said that we were to be given copies of all of the notes that they had given to Baroncourt, as well as the ones that they hadn't. Assuming that it would be those latter which, potentially, would have the most interest *I* would have started my reading with them.

It is probably unnecessary to state that it was not a temptation to which Sherlock Holmes would succumb. Holmes would not even have had the temptation! He began at the beginning and as he very soon started to make extensive notes on his reading, I realised that if the papers did indeed contain the "surprises" which he'd predicted, I might not hear of them for some long time, perhaps not even that day.

My assumption was correct. Holmes was still working when I went to my bed. He was, none the less, at the breakfast table before me. His unmistakably self-satisfied expression suggested that the content of the notes had indeed fulfilled his best expectations – one of those expectations being to prove me wrong about Oldroyd!

"I confess," he began, "to being surprised that Oldroyd's agency managed to do so competent a job in such a comparatively short space of time. Lawrence Oldroyd has nothing of the experience of his father. Either he's been tutored exceptionally well, or his father still takes a much larger hand in the business than he'd have us believe. I'd guess, the latter – but that's not what you're

The Case of the Man who Followed Himself

waiting to hear, is it, Watson?"

Holmes quickly went on to explain that what he had first done, was to break down Oldroyd's notes into what he described as "kinds of incident", attaching to them, where possible, times, dates and places, and then putting them into chronological order.

"Much of the time," he said, "had been spent in interviewing those people who, Baroncourt claimed, had seen him at times and in places where he said he was not. As you would expect, they do all confirm his story. Clearly, the man would not deliberately provide that kind of information falsely, knowing that it could so easily be checked. But such information would only become significant if there were independent evidence that Baroncourt was indeed elsewhere at the times when his double was sighted."

"And there are such instances?" I asked.

"Yes, Watson, several – though if you read my own notes, you will immediately see that none occurs before the time at which Baroncourt engaged the services of Oldroyd and Hughes. I am uncertain of what if any significance that might have. Perhaps only that any earlier instances are not recorded."

"But it does establish that there *are* two of them," I said, "though not that the 'double' is any less flesh and blood than Baroncourt himself."

"Agreed," Holmes answered, "but there is more. There are two reports which apparently establish the truth of Baroncourt's claim that his double had been to places just before him, and at times when he was not yet aware of his own intention to go there. Perhaps I should explain that during the latter part of this investigation, Baroncourt was accompanied, at all times through the day, either by Lawrence Oldroyd and one of his assistants, or by two of the assistants.

"Baroncourt, apparently in order to afford the greatest possible amount of assistance, would provide his planned itinerary for each day, and sometimes for a day or even two days in advance, together with details of whatever flexibility might be possible in changing those arrangements. On two occasions, with Baroncourt's agreement, the place of the intended visit for the afternoon had been changed by Oldroyd over lunch – and was, therefore, known only to Baroncourt and the two who were with him. On both occasions it transpired that the double had been there before them – and on one, was apparently still in the building. Yet no trace of him was found."

"Is this what Oldroyd had omitted from the report?"

"No, Watson. Clearly he couldn't. Baroncourt was already aware of it. The part which was omitted is yet to come. It is but a single incident – though one which you might consider none the less intriguing.

....

Lawrence Oldroyd and an assistant called

The Case of the Man who Followed Himself

Mayhew had arranged to meet Baroncourt at his club at nine thirty one morning. They were on time. Baroncourt was late. As they waited in the entrance hall, they suddenly realised that a stray dog, of a somewhat ferocious and particularly disreputable appearance, had apparently entered with them from the street. The man on duty at the reception desk had, not unnaturally, left the desk to assist in the task of ejecting the animal. It was as they were attempting to do so that Baroncourt had suddenly been seen in that part of the entrance hall which gave the only access to the rest of the club. He could not have just entered from the street without being seen by the others already in the hallway. Nor, it was to transpire, had he been seen entering at any time earlier that morning.

"There is a diagram," Holmes said, "which you will find makes the account easier to follow."

Oldroyd had spoken to the man presumed to be Baroncourt. He'd made no reply, but almost instantly disappeared from view into the corridor which leads, amongst other places, to the members' lounge and dining-room. The dog had followed him, as then did Oldroyd, Mayhew, and Hempson – the man on duty at the desk.

Baroncourt, still followed by the dog, was next seen, running into the members' lounge. Oldroyd, with remarkable foresight in the heat of that moment, instructed Mayhew to remain in the corridor so that there was no possibility of Baron-

A Second Helping

The diagram from Oldroyd's notes

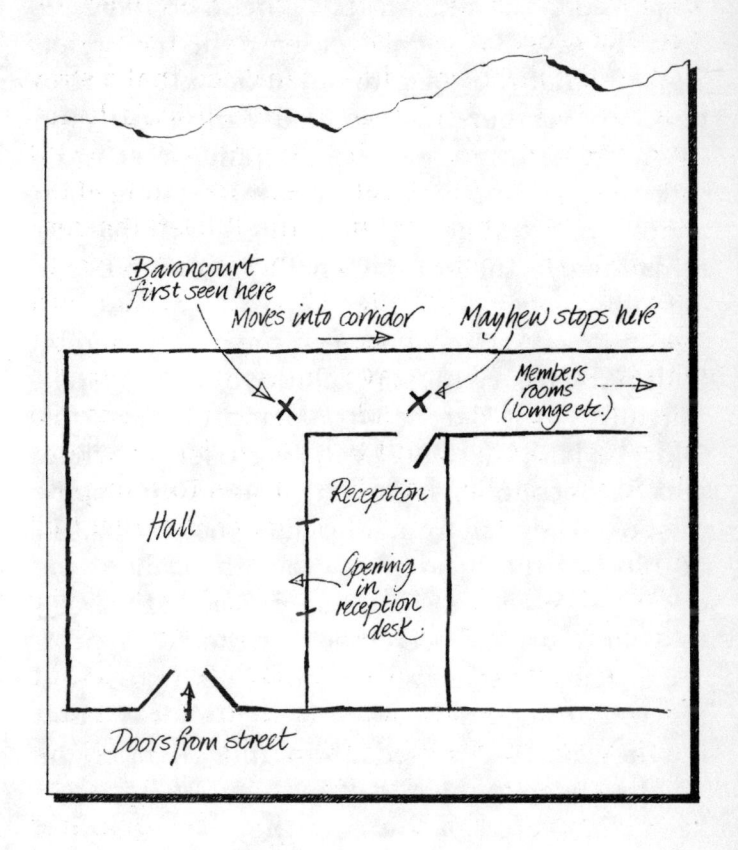

Baroncourt first seen here
Moves into corridor →
Mayhew stops here
Members rooms (lounge etc.) →
Reception
Hall
Opening in reception desk
Doors from street

court – if he it was – from doubling back that way.

Mayhew, from the position in which he had been left standing, could see through the open door of the small room which housed the reception desk, through the opening above the desk,

The Case of the Man who Followed Himself

and into the entrance hall, as far as the doors which led in from the street. As he stood there, he actually saw Baroncourt enter from the street. Sensing that this bizarre situation might prove delicate, Mayhew had greeted Baroncourt, and promptly escorted him back into the street and a little away from the club entrance, telling him about the stray dog and suggesting that by remaining in the entrance hall, they might only get in the way.

Minutes later they had seen the dog ejected by Oldroyd and Hempson. Oldroyd had spotted Mayhew with Baroncourt, Hempson had not. Oldroyd had, therefore been able to join Mayhew and Baroncourt and, correctly interpreting some unspoken signal from Mayhew, had also said nothing of the incident – other than about the dog. The three men had then proceeded directly to wherever it had been their intention to go next.

Consequently, it was at some later time – and not in Baroncourt's presence, that Oldroyd and Mayhew had exchanged information. In brief, the dog had been found and caught, but no trace had been discovered of the man they had followed believing him to be Baroncourt.

"You might say, Watson," Holmes remarked, "that the whole incident illustrates nothing more than another example of what you had already concluded – 'that there are two of them'. But it is Mayhew's addition to the account that makes it much more significant. Mayhew has what the report, using an expression quite new to me, describes as a 'photographic memory'. I take that to mean that he can instantly absorb in his mind every smallest detail – as in a photograph – and recall it, albeit for a short time. His descriptions of the man he first thought to be Baroncourt and the Baroncourt whom he saw entering the club are, therefore, quite remarkable, in more than one respect.

"I will not read you Mayhew's full description but among other things he refers to a scuff mark on the toe of the right shoe, a trace of mud on the bottom of the right trouser leg, the flap of the left jacket pocket turned into the pocket, and a small, but quite inflamed eruption of the skin on the side of the left nostril."

I had to admit that such a degree of observed detail was, indeed, most remarkable.

"Yes, Watson, though I suspect that you are still missing the point! Those details, Mayhew states, were present on *both* men – the one first seen in the entrance hall *and* the one who entered through the doors from the street moments later. Even if these were identical twins, it is impossible to believe that two men could have such unlikely points of identity."

It was, surely, impossible! I did now see why Oldroyd had dropped the case. I still could not bring myself to believe in wafts but, at that moment, I could see no better explanation!"

Chapter Four

Death of a Ghost

I felt that Holmes was again being less than helpful though, for once, perhaps not unreasonably so. He obviously remained unconvinced that Baroncourt's double was any kind of supernatural manifestation, but was offering no explanations for the contents of Oldroyd's report. He would say only that he first needed the answers to several questions – answers which Oldroyd could most probably provide. But today was Sunday and the matter did not appear to be of such urgency that it could not wait until tomorrow. Baroncourt himself had been uncertain of what time he might need to spend in Hadleigh but had promised to contact Holmes immediately upon his return.

I had, therefore, no alternative but to resign myself to waiting – at least until the next day. The matter had not, however, strayed far from the

Death of a Ghost

forefront of my mind and this became apparent when, very late that evening, there was a ring at the front door bell. My instant reaction was to suppose that our caller was Baroncourt, returned from Suffolk, and with some yet stranger sequel to recount.

In the latter part of that assumption, it might be said that I was close to the truth, but our caller was not Baroncourt. It was Chief Inspector Alec Macdonald who we had last seen only upon the previous day when we left him at Scotland Yard. Macdonald described his visit as "semi-official".

"Official," he said, "in the sense that I *have* volunteered to make an official enquiry on behalf of a colleague. Unofficial, in the sense that the principal reason for my being here is simply to satisfy my curiosity. Even without knowing your public reputation, Holmes, our past associations would have been enough to convince me that you do have a nose for the slightly bizarre. What brings me here tonight, I would have to describe as rather more than 'slightly' bizarre. Double killings are not that unusual. But they are when one of the victims is a ghost!"

....

I will not attempt to recount all of the actual conversation which took place that evening, but only to summarise much of Macdonald's extraordinary account of the events of that day.

For Macdonald, it had begun with a routine enquiry to Scotland Yard from the Buckingham-

The Case of the Man who Followed Himself

shire police. It was no more than fortuitous, that Macdonald should have been in "The Yard" at just the time that the message was received, that he should have seen the message, noticed the name of Sherlock Holmes, and noticed also that the originator of the message was an Inspector Tripp – Macdonald's old sergeant in the days when he was still plain "Inspector". It was a combination of circumstances, sufficient to prompt Macdonald into making further enquiries – enquiries which had led to his undertaking an unofficial journey out of London, and a journey from which he had just returned. The place he had been visiting was Selsdon Park!

....

On the previous day, Julius Baroncourt had received at his lodging in the Edgware Road a letter from his uncle Silas. He said that Julius had been seen in the vicinity of Selsdon Park earlier that week, and expressed annoyance that Julius had not thought to visit the house, particularly in view of his stated intention not to pay his usual visit on the coming Sunday. Baroncourt had, at first, dismissed the letter as being no more than a ruse – not untypical of his uncle – and most obviously calculated to cause him to change his mind about paying his usual Sunday visit.

For reasons which the reader will understand, that initial dismissal of the letter as pure invention on the part of Silas Baroncourt was soon to be replaced by a growing sense of misgiving. Julius

Death of a Ghost

Baroncourt's double had never appeared, to his knowledge, anywhere other than in London – but was there any reason to be certain that he had not, or might not, appear in some other place? Baroncourt's doubts had been sufficient to prevent him from leaving for his visit to Hadleigh on Saturday. A sleepless and troubled night had served to convince him that he would have no peace of mind, at least upon the truth of the letter, unless he did, indeed, visit Selsdon Park.

He'd travelled on his usual train, changing at High Wycombe and arriving at Selsdon Halt a little before ten. He had then walked the mile across the fields to the estate. Having his own keys, he'd let himself into the house and was about to call out to his uncle when he'd heard what was, unmistakably, a pistol shot. He'd identified the sound as coming from the study, a room leading directly off the hallway. Thoughtless, at that moment, for his own safety, he'd run towards the study door but, just as he'd reached it, the study door had opened and a man had emerged. Baroncourt, being unable to stop himself in time, the two men had collided.

At this point in the story, a part which only Baroncourt himself could have told, there is some degree of uncertainty. Baroncourt's recollection was not clear. He believed that the only things of which he was in that instant conscious were, first, that the man with whom he had collided was holding a still smoking pistol, and second, a

The Case of the Man who Followed Himself

sudden fear for his own life. There had followed, a desperate struggle. During that struggle, the pistol had gone off for a second time. The intruder had fallen to the floor. Only at that moment, in Baroncourt's recollection, did he become aware that the man now lying upon the floor had every appearance of being himself!

"The uncle, Silas Baroncourt, was also dead?" I asked.

"Very dead, Doctor," Macdonald answered. "A single bullet through the heart and, from the powder burns on the clothing, fired at point blank range."

"And the exact nature of the fatal injury to the other man?" Holmes enquired.

"The bullet entered beneath the lower jaw, travelled almost vertically through the head and exited at the top of the skull. It's messy, Holmes. The gun must have been only inches away when it fired. And before you ask it, 'Yes,' the injury is completely consistent with the gun being fired during a struggle."

"And how was the whole incident discovered – so quickly?"

"Baroncourt returned to Selsdon and reported it to the village constable. There was blood on his clothing and he was understandably distraught but, I gather, quite lucid. The constable, realising it was something well beyond his competance, lost no time in contacting the County police. Tripp was sent to take charge of the investigation."

Death of a Ghost

Macdonald had heard an account from Inspector Tripp, that must have been almost identical to that which Baroncourt had himself related to us only two days before – even to the incident of the double having shaved off his moustache in response to Baroncourt's having done the same.

"Perhaps you have not seen the body," Holmes remarked, "but I should be interested to know whether, like Baroncourt, there was evidence of a moustache, recently removed."

"There was," Macdonald replied, "and I have seen the body – and Baroncourt. And the resemblance really is quite remarkable. See the two together and you can notice small differences but, seen apart, one could easily be mistaken for the other."

"At no time," Holmes observed, "have you referred to this double by a name. I assume, therefore, that his identity remains unknown."

"There were various items on the body, some papers, but nothing that I think will give us a name."

"The clothes?" Holmes asked.

"Odd, that. The clothes on the body were Baroncourt's – taken, Baroncourt said, from the few clothes which he keeps in a wardrobe in the house so that he has a change of clothing there should he ever need it."

"Then the man must have changed in the house. What happened to the original clothes?"

"They were there, thrown on the floor by the

The Case of the Man who Followed Himself

wardrobe, all cheap mass-produced garments, making it impossible to identify either the seller or the purchaser."

The questioning and answering continued for some time, all of the questions asked by Holmes. It is perhaps sufficient that I record its conclusion.

"Tripp is satisfied, and I would have to agree, that on the basis of the evidence so far available there is nothing to disprove Baroncourt's story – that an intruder, bearing a quite astonishing likeness to himself, breaks into Silas Baroncourt's house, dresses in Julius Baroncourt's clothes, kills Silas Baroncourt, and is himself killed as Julius Baroncourt struggles with him in an attempt to wrest the murder weapon from his hand."

"Equally," Holmes said, "I presume that there is no evidence to prove that Julius Baroncourt did not deliberately murder both his uncle and the intruder."

"Precisely, Holmes, which is why I am here – officially, merely to ask you to confirm that Julius Baroncourt did retain your services. That I now know to be so."

"And unofficially?"

"Unofficially, to ask whether you have formed any opinions about this extraordinary affair, given, I know, that your acquaintance with the case has been little longer than forty-eight hours."

If Macdonald was awaiting Holmes' reply with some eagerness, it can have been no greater than my own. It was certain that Holmes *had* formed opinions. He had acquainted me with only one – that Baroncourt's double was *not* supernatural. And that was a matter no longer in any doubt! But, much as I shared Macdonald's hope that I was about to learn more, all that I did, in fact, share with him was disappointment!

"As you say," Holmes observed, "the case has been with me for only two days. I have heard Baroncourt's story, as have you. You must also be aware that he employed the services of Oldroyd and Hughes. I have read the account of their investigation. But you are probably also aware that the investigation was never completed, Baroncourt being no longer able to afford their fees."

"Tripp will, no doubt also wish to read that account but, Holmes, from what you've read –"

"I can tell you nothing, other than that it would appear to establish that Baroncourt did have a double who had for some time been frequenting places that he himself frequented. It suggested no motive for that behaviour."

Macdonald made no attempt to disguise his disappointment at the answer he'd received, but perhaps saw other ways of enlisting Holmes' services.

"You appreciate that I have no official standing in this case, but I can tell you that Inspector Tripp has always been one of your greatest admirers. I'm certain that he would welcome the assistance of your special talents in resolving this mystery –

The Case of the Man who Followed Himself

for mystery it surely is. If it were your wish, I feel certain that something could be arranged . . ."

"It is not my wish," Holmes answered. "I do appreciate the kindness of the thought, but I am involved with other pressing matters. Baroncourt thrust himself upon me at a most inconvenient moment. I am, in truth, grateful that today's developments have put the affair firmly into the hands of the police, and out of mine!"

....

It was not until Macdonald had left that I felt able to speak my mind.

"Holmes," I said, "I've never seen you act like this before. You have what you yourself admitted to being a most puzzling and remarkable case, even before today's still more extraordinary events. Macdonald has offered you an unexpected opportunity to continue your investigation of it. Yet you refuse the offer. Even what you told Macdonald was untrue. There is much more in Oldroyd's report than you suggested. You didn't even tell him that you still had it in your possession. As to your 'other pressing matters', you were complaining, earlier this week, that nothing had recently come your way really worthy of investigation."

"I'm sorry that you are so obviously disappointed in me, Watson. But I didn't tell Macdonald anything untrue. I merely omitted to give him certain pieces of information. I did not say that I did not have Oldroyd's report – and it is my

Death of a Ghost

intention to return it to him early tomorrow morning. In view of the content of that report, I feel that Lawrence Oldroyd and his father might wish to reconsider their conclusions. It might not have been given to me in its present form, had they known that it was likely to be presented in evidence at a coroner's court. As to 'pressing matters', it is some long time since I brought my files up to date."

....

Holmes left the house early next morning, returning just moments after I had myself come down to breakfast. He said only that he had been returning Oldroyd's report. I still could not believe that he had lost all interest in the Baroncourt case but, as the days passed, he gave no indication that it was otherwise. He did, indeed, set about a complete overhaul of his files, something I could not remember him doing before, at least with such a sustained effort. He did, from time to time, leave the house upon errands, the nature of which he chose not to disclose to me, but that was, for Sherlock Holmes, quite normal behaviour. I did, upon several occasions, attempt to raise the Baroncourt affair, but got no other response than that I could readily satisfy my curiosity merely by following the reports in the newspapers.

....

The inquest was opened and adjourned, a formality necessary to allow the burial of the bodies. The full hearing of the evidence did not occur for a further three weeks. Holmes was not called as a witness. Having provided a written deposition stating that Baroncourt had sought to enlist his services, I supposed that he could rightly claim to be unable to offer any evidence not already contained in Baroncourt's statement to the police and the report of the investigation carried out by Oldroyd and Hughes.

I had assumed that the reports of the inquest would be highly sensational. I was therefore surprised and, I would have to say, disappointed that they were not – at least not nearly to the degree that I would have anticipated. And I speak not merely of the restrained reporting associated with the columns of *The Times*, but of the several more popular newspapers, often given to wild excesses in their desire to provide their readers with a "good story".

With two deaths, under what were the most unusual of circumstances, the reports could hardly fail to be dramatic. Yet nothing emerged in the evidence which even suggested that certain aspects of the behaviour of Baroncourt's double were totally inexplicable, much less that they might be seen as supernatural. The emphasis was much more upon sympathy for Baroncourt – the subject of a long series of "apparently deliberate and frightening impersonations", culminating in the murder of his uncle and, it was assumed, the intended murder of himself. Baroncourt was presented as a man brought by these terrible experiences to the verge of total mental and physical collapse, who had given his evidence in "little more than a whisper" and had, twice during the hearing, required medical attention. In his summing up to the jury, the coroner had referred to Baroncourt's remarkable bravery in attempting to overcome an armed intruder in his concern for his uncle's safety.

The verdict on Silas Baroncourt was, therefore, as could have been predicted – "murder by a person, identity unknown". That on the unknown man, killed during the struggle, I found surprising – "death by misadventure".

"Why 'surprising'?" Holmes asked. "What had you been expecting?"

"Manslaughter," I answered.

"No, Watson. Causing the death of another by accident is not of necessity, manslaughter. One has to apply the principle of *'mens rea'* that is whether the person has a 'guilty mind', or to put it in more practical terms, whether that person is guilty of negligence or mental inadvertance. The jury obviously considered Baroncourt to be guilty of neither. The verdict is therefore a sound one."

"Then what happens now?" I asked, "to Baroncourt, I mean."

"I would expect, nothing. A verdict of either murder or manslaughter would have required the coroner to have issued a warrant for Baroncourt's arrest. But 'death by misadventure' will almost

The Case of the Man who Followed Himself

certainly mean that he goes free. It is what I had hoped."

For the second time in a month, Holmes had left me totally confounded. I had been at a complete loss to understand his ready abandonment of the case. Now he appeared to be expressing satisfaction with what amounted to a 'not guilty' verdict, when he had at least hinted at the possibility that Baroncourt might be guilty of double murder! The news of the verdicts had been too late for the evening newspapers and the conversation I have just described had taken place over breakfast. The occasion had provided me with one surprise, but there was to be another.

Holmes suddenly got up from the breakfast table and went into his bedroom. He emerged moments later, minus his dressing-gown and apparently dressed to go out.

"I have to leave you," he said, "but am assuming that you can make yourself available to assist me later this morning. Let us say, eleven thirty."

"Yes," I said. "Where?"

"Boul's Club in York Street," he answered. "If I am not there, Chief Inspector Macdonald will be waiting for you in the hallway."

Chapter Five

Unsupported Evidence

Following his unexpected announcement of the meeting at Boul's Club, Holmes had promptly left the house, leaving me in no possible doubt that both his announcement and departure were deliberately timed to prevent my asking any of the dozen questions that now filled my mind. The time being then only nine thirty, I had fully two hours in which to ponder those questions for myself but when, at some two minutes to the appointed hour, my cab drew up outside Boul's, though the questions remained, none was accompanied by any answer – at least of a kind to which I could give much credence.

Holmes was not in the hallway of the club as I entered. Alec Macdonald was, and accompanied by a man whom I did not recognise though, from the alpaca jacket which he was wearing, I took him to be one of the club's employees. Macdonald

The Case of the Man who Followed Himself

introduced him as "Hempson".

"Ah!" I said, "you were the man on duty at the desk when . . ."

Macdonald correctly interpreted the reason for my sudden hesitation.

"It's all right, Doctor. I do know the story. I have read Oldroyd's report, including that part of it which was not handed over to Baroncourt, and which our friend Holmes still had in his possession on the night I visited you at Baker Street."

I was saved from what I saw as the possible embarrassment of having to respond to that information by Macdonald's suddenly turning away from me, directing his attention towards the back of the hallway. Very naturally, I followed his gaze – to see that Holmes was standing there, near to the corridor which led from the hallway to the rest of the building.

"Here's Holmes now," I said.

"You're quite sure that that is Holmes?" was Macdonald's surprising question.

"Of course I am! I *have* known the man for seventeen years, and shared lodgings with him for ten. I'm not likely to be mistaken!"

I'd hardly said the words before Holmes stepped out of the hallway and into the corridor, and was, consequently, no longer in sight.

"Then let's see if you're right!" Macdonald declared, instantly moving off in the direction which Holmes had taken. I followed, as did Hempson.

I reached the corridor in time to see Holmes,

Unsupported Evidence

Illustration from James Bradwell's London's Clubs, *published by Seligman and Harz, 1902.*

The Entrance Hall of Boul's

The Case of the Man who Followed Himself

perhaps twenty yards ahead of us, and just about to enter through one of the several doorways. I'd taken no more than another two or three steps, before Macdonald grabbed my arm.

"Look!" he said.

We had stopped in the corridor by the open door of the reception desk. Macdonald was pointing towards the opening in the desk, through which it was possible to see into the hallway which we had just left. I could see someone coming in through the street doors. It was Holmes!

....

It will require little reflection on the part of the reader to realise that what I had just seen enacted had been arranged with the full knowledge and cooperation of the club's secretary. It was he who escorted Holmes, Macdonald and myself to a small private room, I assumed for the purpose of my being offered some explanation!

"I apologise," Holmes began, "for certain obvious omissions in my reconstruction – like the presence of a stray mongrel dog. On the first occasion, it was a necessary addition, merely to ensure that Hempson left his desk and came into the hallway. In this instance he did so by prior arrangement with myself. You must also accept my word that the man who you saw in the corridor, about to enter the members' lounge, could have left the building by a window which leads into a yard, and from which, by way of a passage, it is possible to reach Jermyn Street."

Unsupported Evidence

"You are saying, Holmes," I interrupted, "that the man I first saw in the hallway, was *not* you!"

"No, Watson. That *was* me. But before we go further, let me introduce the man who you saw entering the lounge."

Holmes crossed to the door of the room and opened it. The man who entered was dressed like Holmes, but there was little other resemblance. He was tall, but not as tall as Holmes, and he was certainly a deal more solidly built.

"But he's nothing like you!" I said.

"Let me quote you, Watson," Holmes replied. "'It's a classic case of mistaken identity, often based upon a quite fleeting glimpse of someone who, in truth, bears little real resemblance to oneself'. You said it to Baroncourt when he first quoted an example of the appearance of his double in the streets. In fairness to you Watson, the deception in this case was considerably aided by the corridor being relatively ill lit and quite shadowy. Constable Burke was the nearest our friend, Chief Inspector Macdonald, could find to someone of my build – though you must admit that the resemblance proved adequate enough."

I could do no other than agree. But if the man I'd seen in the corridor was not Holmes, but the man I'd seen in the hallway was, then how had Holmes managed to vanish, only to appear, seconds later, entering from the street!

"A piece of careful timing," Holmes answered. "There were two of us in the corridor, myself and

The Case of the Man who Followed Himself

Constable Burke. I showed myself briefly, then stepped back out of sight. Constable Burke began walking down the corridor. I slipped into the room which houses the reception desk. As the three of you reached the corridor and turned the corner, I vaulted over the desk into the hallway and left through the front doors – immediately returning, and so giving the impression that I had just entered the club from the street."

Macdonald left the club with his constable and I with Holmes.

....

Having now had time to give more careful thought to what I had just seen in Boul's, a number of other questions occurred to me – questions and their answers which occupied the whole of the return cab journey to Baker Street and were still continuing when we entered our living room.

"Accept, Watson," Holmes said, "that I cannot satisfy you upon every detail – like when and how Baroncourt and his double entered the club, and how they succeeded in avoiding being seen together. There must have been a considerable element of luck for them to have achieved the success that they did. The use of the stray dog to entice Hempson from his desk could so easily have gone wrong – if, for instance, Oldroyd and Mayhew had succeeded in quickly ejecting it.

"But I would submit that none of that is of great account. The fact remains that I have demonstrated one means by which the incident recounted in Oldroyd's report does not require any supernatural explanation. I have never doubted it. Having rejected the idea of the supernatural, only one explanation of Mayhew's identical description of the 'two' men, was possible. They were not two men, but the same man!"

Despite the fact that my natural curiosity had prompted me to probe into so many details, ever since leaving the club, I had entertained no real doubts that Holmes' explanation was something very close to the truth.

"But you must know," I said, "that it's an explanation which is only possible if there was, in fact, deliberate and calculated collusion between Baroncourt and his double."

"I am aware of it, and I am in no doubt that it is true. You see, Watson, once you have made that assumption, there are no more mysteries – at least not regarding anything contained in Oldroyd's report. For reasons which I shall explain, it was necessary that you should believe that I had dropped the Baroncourt case. I admit that there were several limitations to the amount of investigation that I, Macdonald, or Inspector Tripp, could carry out without drawing unwanted attention to our activities, but there are things which I can now tell you.

"You will recall two instances in Oldroyd's report where Baroncourt's double appeared in places, before him, and at times when it would appear that even Baroncourt could not have

The Case of the Man who Followed Himself

known that he was about to visit those places. I told you at the time that I needed to have the answers to some questions. I did obtain them.

"If you were to visit Hoxton's toy shop in the Baker Street Bazaar, I have no doubt that you could purchase a pack of playing cards which would guarantee your ability to predict any card which might be chosen from it."

"Either," I said, "because the cards are secretly marked on the backs, or every card is the same!"

"The latter, Watson – a child's conjuring trick. Yet one not immediately recognised when placed in an unfamiliar setting. Baroncourt had offered a choice of no less than four places which he, Oldroyd and Mayhew might visit that afternoon. Oldroyd made the choice of which. It transpired that Baroncourt's double had visited the place that morning. Baroncourt feigned such distress at the discovery that he found himself 'unable' to continue with the afternoon's itinerary."

"Though, if he had, it would have been discovered that his double had been to every one of the four places!"

"Correct, Watson. But the good conjurer does not employ the same method twice. On the second occasion, the choice was a genuine one. Baroncourt had, therefore, secretly to pass the information to his double, during lunch. That was why the double had just arrived at the building before them, and was still supposed to be in it when they arrived. He had, of course, already left by some means, other than the front door. Unless a building is a bank or a prison, there are, invariably, several ways of leaving it, unobserved.

"The rest, Watson, I'm sure that you can explain yourself."

"You mean that whenever Baroncourt wished to be seen in some place where he was not, he merely used his double?"

"Only, it seems, in that period after he had hired Oldroyd and Hughes to carry out their investigation. For most of the time, it was even simpler than that. Julius Baroncourt acted as his own double. He would, for example, visit his own club, speak to no-one, do nothing, and then leave. He would then return at some later time, claiming that to be the first visit. He did speak the truth when he said, speaking of his double, 'it is as if it is *I* who follow him'. Indeed it was!"

I asked Holmes for how long he had known, or perhaps guessed at, what he had told me.

"Since Baroncourt's visit to Baker Street," he answered. "I knew then that it was unlikely that he was telling the truth. He told us that he did some of his business by correspondence and that he needed his club to provide him with a 'respectable address'. He also said that he visited his club upon most days to collect letters.

"Remember now what he told us about his double, who obviously did enter by the front door! He said that his double was admitted because he was taken to be himself. Finally, he in-

The Case of the Man who Followed Himself

sisted that his double always appeared before him. Whatever time he visited his club, his double had been there earlier.

"I know Watson, that you are not an enthusiastic 'club man', but let me ask you this. Upon entering such an establishment, having been identified and greeted by the man at reception, what might you expect to happen next?"

It took me a moment's thought to reply.

"I would be handed any letters or messages which had been left for me."

"Precisely, Watson. So why was Baroncourt's double never given Baroncourt's letters? Perhaps it was yet another of his 'supernatural' attributes only to arrive on days when there were no letters. In a sense, Watson, that *is* the explanation. Only on those days did Baroncourt decide to play his double – speaking to no-one, and arriving for a second time in that day, claiming not to have been there before!"

It was not a new experience for me to find, having listened to one of Sherlock Holmes' 'explanations', that I was left feeling that it had raised even more questions than it had supplied answers – and never more so than at that moment!

Holmes had at least suspected that Baroncourt was lying since that first meeting. Though he had arranged the demonstration only that morning he had known about the whole of Baroncourt's deception, I imagined, for some time. Certainly prior to the inquest verdicts. He had implied that

Unsupported Evidence

that knowledge was shared with Chief Inspector Macdonald and Inspector Tripp.

Sherlock Holmes had suggested in my presence that the deaths of Silas Baroncourt and the 'intruder', could have been murder, and the double murderer none other than Julius Baroncourt. What he had just told me seemed to make that a much more likely possibility. Yet Holmes had offered no such evidence at the inquests. Nor had Inspector Tripp – at least of a kind that would have cast serious doubt upon a verdict of "death by misadventure".

All of this I said to Holmes – though probably at much greater length. He took the time to fill and light his pipe before attempting to reply. "The way you say it, Watson, you make it all sound like a conspiracy to pervert the course of justice!"

I began to stammer some denial.

"No apology is necessary. You might well see it in that light, but only if you are missing one vitally important fact. Everything that I've told you about Baroncourt I am certain to be the truth – including his being guilty of a double murder. But I can prove none of it. Those parts of Oldroyd's investigation which suggested some supernatural element were not offered at the inquest merely because subsequent events had proved them to be patently untrue, and therefore irrelevant.

"But I do see what you are thinking. If those parts of the evidence had not been omitted, and I had offered the explanation which I have offered

The Case of the Man who Followed Himself

to you, then the verdict might have been different – possibly, 'murder'. But, I repeat, Watson – my testimony would have been unsupported evidence, indeed, mere speculation. For that reason, the coroner would most certainly have ruled it as inadmissible. Oldroyd would have been made to look foolish, but without my testimony, I doubt whether the verdict would have changed. In the event, the verdict is a most satisfactory one."

It was the second time that day that Holmes had expressed satisfaction with the verdict of 'death by misadventure'. I still did not understand why.

"I've told you, Watson. A verdict of murder or manslaughter would have meant that Baroncourt would be tried upon one of those charges. And he would be found 'not guilty'."

"You seem very certain, Holmes."

"I am, Watson. In an English court, the burden of proof lies with the prosecution. There is no 'proof'. But there is a great deal of 'reasonable doubt'. In fact, Watson, there is very little about this case which would seem to make any sense at all. In such circumstances a jury would have to find the accused 'not guilty'. Indeed, if Baroncourt were to retain a skilful barrister, a man with the reputation of Edward Marshall Hall, his case would be won before he ever stepped into court."

I was still puzzled. Either way, it would appear that Baroncourt ended up a free man.

"No, Watson. A man tried and found not guilty cannot be tried again for the same offence. Baron-

Unsupported Evidence

court does not yet enjoy that immunity."

"You're suggesting, Holmes, that Baroncourt might still be brought to trial. But there would be little point in that unless, as you say, there were clear proof of his guilt. You say there is none."

"Say rather, Watson, that there is none – yet."

I could accept the idea that Holmes had every intention of pursuing the investigation. I could not see in what direction. I assumed that Holmes and the police between them had already pursued every possible line of enquiry.

"As I see it," I said, "there is only one person left who knows the truth – and that's Baroncourt. And *he* is hardly likely to assist you!"

Holmes knocked out the ash from his pipe into the empty grate.

"Not willingly, Watson. Certainly not willingly. I said that I had a reason for keeping you in ignorance of any of the investigations which I carried out, prior to the inquest verdicts. You came near to guessing that reason for yourself when, in as many words, you suggested that there might have been a conspiracy to pervert the course of justice. I assure you that there was not, but the situation was, at times, delicate. Accusations might have been made – even falsely. I did not wish you to be involved. But that time is over.

"You have rightly said that there remains only one useful source of information – Julius Baroncourt. I trust, Watson, that I can rely upon you to help me in persuading him to reveal it!"

Chapter Six

Deceptive Appearances

The next day, Holmes having assured me that he was unlikely to be needing my services, I left the house around mid-morning for the purpose of visiting Trumpers in Curzon Street to have a much needed haircut. I returned well before noon only to find that Holmes had also left the house. Mrs Hudson was unable to tell me where he had gone but she thought that it might have some connection with someone he had seen from the window.

She, Mrs Hudson, had been tidying the room, "as much, that is, Doctor Watson, as I'm ever allowed – which is not much more than dusting around Mr Holmes's clutter. Mr Holmes is standing at the window, looking down into the street, when he says, 'That's —'." She paused. "I did know the name – that young man who came to the door all upset and wanting to see Mr Holmes – it must be a month or more since. I'm remembering it was a hot day and me in the middle of baking . . ."

"Baroncourt," I said.

"That was it – Mr Baroncourt."

"And then?" I asked.

"Well nothing, really," was the infuriatingly unhelpful reply. "As I said, Mr Holmes said, 'That's Mr Baroncourt'. He might not have said 'Mr'. And then he went out. And that must be an hour since."

It was, I thought, typical of my frequent misfortunes that the occasion when I had left the house for what was, I suppose, a trifling purpose, should be the very time for Baroncourt to put in a mysterious and quite unexpected appearance. I could do no other than wait for Holmes' return – which was almost an hour later.

He seemed well enough pleased, though I saw no reason for it. I thought his news disappointing. He had, as Mrs Hudson had told me, seen Baroncourt in the street, crossing from the opposite side of the road towards 221B. When he had passed from sight below the window, Holmes had naturally assumed that it was his intention to call. But, when neither knock on the door nor ring at the bell had followed, it seemed that the man had, for some reason, changed his mind. Holmes had gone down to the street, but Baroncourt was not even in sight.

"It seemed like an opportunity, Watson, that

The Case of the Man who Followed Himself

should not be missed. It did appear that he had at least contemplated calling here. If Baroncourt was in London, then there were two places to which he might have gone – his club or, a lesser possibility, the room which he had in the Edgware Road. I went first to his club – not, I may say, without what seems to be the ever worsening problem of delays caused by the sheer volume of traffic. In direct consequence of that, though I had gone to the right place, I missed him again. He had left moments before my arrival. You may have guessed that my visit to the Edgware Road was no more successful. His visit there had been, it seems, even more fleeting than that to his club. His landlady had seen him leaving – too late to have had any opportunity to speak to him. The rent of his room is paid in advance until the end of this week. Naturally, she is anxious to know whether he wishes to retain it after that time. I know that I might then have gone to Paddington Station – but I did not."

"Then you should be disappointed," I said. "But you don't appear to be."

"I'm not – not too disappointed. I think that we have still been provided with the opportunity I was seeking, a means of obtaining an invitation to Selsdon Park."

....

Holmes sat himself down after lunch and penned a letter to Baroncourt. He began by setting out the events of that morning which he had related to me, following it with the suggestion that while he had no wish to appear to be pressing his services, should there be any way in which he might still offer help, he would do so most willingly.

I thought that Holmes might be being rather too optimistic. Admittedly, Baroncourt had come to Baker Street – but had clearly changed his mind. I saw nothing in Holmes' letter which I felt was guaranteed to make him change it again.

Holmes did not share my opinion. "Not only," he said, "will Baroncourt reply favourably, but he will do so by telegram."

The telegram arrived on the following afternoon! At eleven next morning, Holmes and I were disembarking from the train at Selsdon Halt.

....

Selsdon Halt was a small and obviously quiet station, so it was perhaps no surprise that on leaving it we could see no kind of transport for hire. It being yet another fine, sunny day but with a pleasantly cool breeze blowing from the northwest, Holmes decided that we should walk to Selsdon Park, across the fields. He bade me stay where I was, whilst he returned to the station to enquire of the porter the direction which we should take.

From a distance, Selsdon Park House was not unimposing though, as we approached, the neglect of which Baroncourt had told us became increasingly apparent. The bell on the door was broken, the pull hanging loosely from its socket,

The Case of the Man who Followed Himself

suspended by a foot of rusted wire. A deal of hammering on the cracked and peeling door itself, eventually brought a response. The door was opened by Baroncourt himself.

He was profuse in his apologies that he had been unable to make any arrangements for us to be met from the train. Holmes *had* telegraphed a reply to Baroncourt's telegram giving the time of our arrival at Selsdon Halt.

"My uncle's estate is considerable," he said, "but obtaining probate will take some time. I have obtained a loan to meet my immediate needs, but not of sufficient size to feel that I can yet employ a full-time staff. I have a man and his wife who are acting as handyman-gardener and cook-housekeeper but, other than a little part-time help from the village, that is all. You have only to look at the place to see the work which it requires, but it will take time and I have not been at all well, since that dreadful day that . . . Forgive me. I have no wish to burden you with such matters as my state of health."

Baroncourt did not *look* physically ill, but he was in a state of considerable nervous agitation.

"I did know that you'd been unwell," Holmes told him. "Naturally, I read the reports of the inquest, – and I gathered that you were still not fully recovered. The station porter who directed us here remarked upon it. I understand that he saw you on your return from your recent visit to London."

Deceptive Appearances

Baroncourt had been escorting us across the hall, presumably with the intention of taking us to some place where we might talk in comfort. Quite suddenly, he stopped and, turning to Holmes, asked, "Are you certain that he was not referring to some other occasion?"

Holmes assured him that he was not mistaken. The man had said, "day afore yesterday". We moved on, but the incident struck me as odd.

Perhaps it was no more odd than the conversation which was to follow in the next hour. It began with Baroncourt's explaining his purpose in inviting us to Selsdon Park.

"In one way, Mr Holmes, Dr Watson, it might be said that it is a nightmare which is over – and therefore best forgotten. I have new responsibilities – the means and the desire to restore this house and the estate – matters more than sufficient to occupy my mind and help me not to dwell upon things past. Yet I am far from certain that that is possible.

"I have no need to tell you, gentlemen, that I first came to you with a disturbing mystery. Subsequent events have not solved that mystery. They have only deepened it! I did say that it might be seen as a nightmare which is over – but my fear is that it is not!"

"You must explain," Holmes told him.

"When we first talked, I told you that I could see no motive for the behaviour of my double. You might say that that is no longer true. I cannot vouch for the truth of it, but I can see only one explanation. This man who could be taken for myself, had planned first to murder my uncle, then to take my place. If I also were dead, then he could claim that it was I who was the double, and that it was I, the double, who had murdered Silas Baroncourt. I can only thank Heaven that something went wrong with his plan. I told you that I had little affection for my uncle, but I could wish that he too had escaped the fate which was meant for both of us."

"Good Heavens!" I exclaimed. "That thought had never occurred to me."

"It was an obvious possibility," Holmes answered, "the truth of which must remain as speculation. But you have not yet told me your reason for supposing that the matter is not at an end."

"I said that the mystery had deepened, Mr Holmes, and indeed it has. If the motive which I have just suggested is true, it does not seem to offer any clear reason for all of the strange events which went before. Nor have some of them been explained – unless my double had some help. I'm sorry, Mr Holmes. I am confused in my mind. I think that what I am trying to say is, 'Was there more than one person involved in a plot to murder both my uncle and myself?'. And if that is true, am I still in some kind of danger?"

"And you wish me to discover the truth of that?" Holmes questioned.

Deceptive Appearances

"I don't know, Mr Holmes. I came to Baker Street and, as you know, changed my mind, and left without calling upon you. When I invited you here, I confess to having changed my mind again. Now, I am once again uncertain. I still need more time to think. I am sorry for having wasted your journey and your time. I will, of course, pay for it."

Holmes dismissed the idea of any payment, saying that he fully understood Baroncourt's indecision. The conversation had been so unlike anything I might have expected, I had almost forgotten the true purpose of our visit – in Holmes' words, to "persuade" Baroncourt to confess to a double murder! Baroncourt had insisted that we at least take tea with him before we leave, and it was served, minutes later, by a woman who I took to be his cook-housekeeper. I thought this, perhaps, would be the opportunity for Holmes to use the more relaxed atmosphere to trap Baroncourt into making some slip. But again I was wrong. Baroncourt continued to do most of the talking, showing, I thought, an unusual interest in Holmes' account of his failure to catch up with him in London, two days later. The tea drunk, the visit then ended and we were returning across the fields to the railway station!

....

Even without the benefit of my long experience of the behaviour of Sherlock Holmes, my readers may not be surprised, when I say that he flatly

The Case of the Man who Followed Himself

refused to discuss the afternoon's conversation – other than to assure me that he had found the occasion to have been "rewarding" even beyond his expectations. He did add, I suppose by way of what he considered some explanation, that his silence upon the matter was "necessary", adding that he did not anticipate that it would be too long before my natural curiosity could be satisfied.

My own impressions of the meeting were, first, that I had begun to wonder whether Baroncourt might not be telling the truth and, second, that Holmes had made no effort to achieve what he had clearly stated to be the purpose of our visit. His assertion that the meeting had been "rewarding" beyond his expectations had only added to my total confusion of mind!

At eight o'clock on the following evening, Baker Street had another late visitor – a police constable bearing a message from Chief Inspector Alec Macdonald. The message was, "He's left Selsdon and is on the train which arrives at Paddington at eight forty-five."

At eight thirty-five, Holmes, myself, and Alec Macdonald, were standing together in a storeroom that overlooked the platform at which the Oxford train would arrive.

"I have four men in plain clothes," Macdonald had explained, "and three cabs. If Baroncourt takes a cab, then two of my cabs will take turns to keep close to him. We will follow in the third. If he walks, then two of my men will follow him in turn. We will follow the man who is farther behind. That way, he's less likely to realise that he's being followed. And he's not going to see any of us – any whom he'd recognise."

The train was late. Holmes had started to show some concern at the fact that, being early September, it was beginning to turn dark. He could obviously not resist the temptation to remind Macdonald that had he been allowed to adopt some appropriate disguise and to follow Baroncourt alone, there would have been less chance of losing him than did now seem possible. It was a matter resolved by the arrival of the train.

Baroncourt left the station and, walking past the line of waiting cabs, made his way into Praed Street. At the junction with the Edgware Road, he turned left. It was still light enough to see the man we were following, but neither Baroncourt, nor the man walking immediately behind him. The man in front of us, suddenly stopped. Macdonald walked on. After a brief word with his plain clothes man he returned to say, "It hasn't worked, Holmes. He's let himself into the house where he rented a room. What do you propose that we should do now?"

"Wait," was Holmes' answer. "And I suggest from the other side of the road. Baroncourt's room is at the front. He will need a light. If we can see it, then when it goes out, we will at least have some forewarning that he is leaving."

By the time we had crossed the road and moved

The Case of the Man who Followed Himself

closer to the house, there was already a light in a third storey window. The curtains were drawn to, but not completely closed, leaving a gap sufficient to see that someone was moving about inside.

I had still been given no indication of why we were here or what was expected to happen. From Alec Macdonald's earlier remark, it seemed, probably nothing – except perhaps a long wait! It was for that reason that I was not intent upon watching the window. Our brief walk along Praed Street had not failed to bring back sad memories of the short but happy time I had spent there in general practice with my beloved Mary, so cruelly taken from me in the flower of her youth. I was, therefore, totally unprepared for the sudden sound of breaking glass and was some moments in realising that it came from the window of the lighted room, the lower pane of the sash window now having in it a large hole – as if some object had been hurled against it from within. Holmes had turned to Macdonald. "No!" he said, "Not yet!"

Lights had appeared in the houses around us – including some in the lower windows of the house which we were watching. Curtains were drawn back. A lull in the traffic, still considerable even late in the evening, brought with it a sudden, eerie stillness. It was a stillness broken by an unmistakable voice, raised as if in anger – or fear! The words were clear –

"Why, Baroncourt? I did no more to you than

Deceptive Appearances

you had planned to do to me." There was a pause, and then, "I told you to stay away from me. You don't frighten me. You're dead – dead and buried! You can't –"

The voice had stopped. I could see movement in the room – shadows on the thin curtains.

"Holmes!" I exclaimed. "There are two of them. I can see –"

A dark shape had come close to the window. And then, slowly, as if someone were pushing it, something came out through the already broken glass. There was a thud on the pavement opposite and a lighter tinkling of broken glass. Now there was nothing at the window – no movement but a slight fluttering of curtains in the night breeze.

....

Holmes and Macdonald were running across the road. I followed. One of Macdonald's men was already hammering upon the front door of the house. The other, I imagined, had been dispatched to the back. Macdonald was bending over the body which lay on the pavement, Holmes held a lantern which illuminated the face. The man was dead. The impossible angle of the head told me that the neck was broken.

"Well," I said, "Baroncourt will tell us nothing now."

"That," Holmes answered, "is certainly true. You see, Watson, Julius Baroncourt died and was buried a month ago, in an unmarked grave. This man is not Julius Baroncourt!"

Chapter Seven

Haunters and the Haunted

It was in the early hours of the following morning that Holmes and I returned to Baker Street. Holmes suggested that faced with a possibly busy day ahead, we might both do well to snatch some sleep in what little of the night remained.

The day *was* busy, Holmes making two visits to Scotland Yard, and Baker Street being visited by both Macdonald and Inspector Tripp who had come up from Buckinghamshire. I did hear the conversation that took place among Holmes, Macdonald and Tripp – at times, making my own small contributions to it. There were even some opportunities for me to ask Holmes at least a few of the many questions that naturally filled my head. I am sure that Holmes did his very best to answer them, yet the effect seemed rather to add to my confusion of mind, than reduce it. I understood that the man who had played the part of

Baroncourt's double had, somehow, turned the tables upon him, not merely taking his place, but very nearly succeeding in inheriting the estate and fortune of the late Silas Baroncourt. What I did not understand was how he could have achieved this without detection, or why the affair had ended as it did. Why had the imposter come to London and what strange things had occurred in that third floor room from which he had fallen to his death?

It was not until we had finished our evening meal and Holmes had settled himself in his chair to enjoy an after-dinner pipe, that he said, "Watson, I am conscious of your anxiety to understand this case and do sense your natural feeling of frustration in not yet doing so. It might help me in explaining this most extraordinary and convoluted of mysteries if I were to give a name to the unknown player, so far variously referred to by such titles as 'Baroncourt's double' or 'the intruder'. I proposed to call him, 'John Smith'."

Since John is my own Christian name, I suggested that we settle for plain 'Mr Smith'.

"As you wish, Watson – and it is with 'plain Mr Smith' that we could even begin. For it was he, on the occasion of our recent visit to Selsdon Park, who came so astonishingly close to recounting the truth of the affair.

"There are some things, Watson, which we shall never know. But we must assume that it

The Case of the Man who Followed Himself

begins with a scheme devised by Baroncourt to murder his uncle and inherit what is obviously a very considerable fortune. We do know that this scheme necessitated his establishing the existence of a double. Much of that, as I have already explained to you, he achieved by himself – even to that point in time where he sought the assistance of the police. He knew, I'm certain, that the police would offer him no help, but the circumstance had now been 'officially' reported.

"Things changed when he decided to enlist the services of Oldroyd and Hughes. He now needed some corroborative evidence of his story. As Smith rightly suggested in our conversation at Selsdon Park, he now needed assistance. It was, of course, Mr Smith himself who provided that assistance.

"And now, we can only speculate – upon two things. Did Baroncourt know, from the very inception of his scheme, of the existence of Mr Smith, a man bearing such a striking resemblance to himself, or was it that discovery which prompted him to go to Oldroyd and Hughes? We shall never know. I believe it to be the former, but it is not important. It is the other thing which is so much more intriguing.

"Most obviously, Baroncourt planned not merely to murder his uncle, but in some way, to use his double to establish his innocence of that murder. We know that he enlisted the services of Mr Smith to play that double. What we do not know, and never can, is *how* he succeeded in enlisting Smith's services. I am not speaking of any payment he must have offered, but of what story he told Smith of the part he was to play in the scheme. We *can* be sure that whatever proposition Baroncourt did put to Smith, it was not one in which Smith was going to prove Baroncourt's innocence of his uncle's murder by ending up dead!"

"You mean," I said, "that Baroncourt's real plan had always required the death of Mr Smith?"

"Yes, Watson. It's logical, for two reasons. It removes the obvious possibility of future blackmail and it would have provided a simple means of overcoming the one important respect in which Baroncourt and Mr Smith were not alike."

"But they were alike," I said, "so far as I could tell – in *every* respect. Macdonald actually saw the two of them together and remarked on the astonishing likeness. You and I, Holmes, have seen both of them – admittedly at different times. But we saw Baroncourt here in Baker Street. You tell me that the man whom we saw at Selsdon Park was Mr Smith. You might say that it's no more than a sad reflection on my powers of observation, but I'll tell you, Holmes, I'd have sworn on oath that they were one and the same person!"

"There is nothing wrong with your powers of observation," Holmes assured me, "but I ask you to let me tell this in my own way. It will all make

The Case of the Man who Followed Himself

sense in the end. Meanwhile, Watson, you must bear with me."

I was well used to doing that! I merely nodded my assent.

"One thing puzzled me from the beginning."

"You mean that you suspected Baroncourt was lying when he came here, but could see no reason for it."

"That's true, Watson, but I assumed that to be a matter which would be resolved in due time. What puzzled me was why, if it was merely Baroncourt's wish to establish the existence of a double, he should have chosen to present it as something apparently supernatural. I cannot, for instance, believe that his intention was to make it appear that his uncle had been murdered by a ghost!

"In fact, it was simple. I should have seen it instantly myself, but it was our conversation with Jack Oldroyd in Simpson's which made me see it. You see, Watson, other than in the case of identical twins, one similarity between two people is very much less common than physical appearance – the voice. But, as Oldroyd told you, 'wafts' don't speak. Baroncourt's double never spoke, not because he was a waft but because he didn't sound like Baroncourt. That is my reason for supposing that Baroncourt knew of Mr Smith's existence from the very beginning of his scheme. And I was reminded of the voice again when I read the reports of the inquest. Remember, Watson, that

Baroncourt gave his evidence 'in little more than a whisper'."

I had perhaps got as far as opening my mouth, but not of saying anything. "'No', Watson!" Holmes interjected. "I know what you're going to say – but don't. Not yet.

"When we were at Selsdon Park, Smith observed that 'something went wrong'. It did, Watson! Either Mr Smith finally realised that he was intended to meet the same fate as Silas Baroncourt, or it was simply that he suddenly saw himself in a position completely to turn the tables on Julius.

"He did exactly what he suggested to us at Selsdon Park. He murdered Silas, took Baroncourt's place, claimed Baroncourt to be the double – and blamed the murder on him. And now, Watson, you have my permission to tell me that I have to be wrong!"

There now seemed little point in doing it. Holmes obviously knew what I was going to say. I had, in fact, already said it – in more general terms. The man I had seen at Baker Street and the man I had seen at Selsdon Park, I would have taken to be the same man, and that included the voice, yet Holmes insisted that the man at Selsdon Park was not Baroncourt, but Smith.

"No, Watson," Holmes said. "You are not being stupid – and I've already told you that, in this instance, there was nothing wrong with your powers of observation. Let me assure you that it

The Case of the Man who Followed Himself

was one aspect of the mystery which placed considerable demands upon my own deductive powers.

"You see, Watson, it was certain that the purpose of Baroncourt's visit to the police, and his employment of Oldroyd and Hughes was merely to establish the apparent truth of his story about his double. When you read Oldroyd's report, you are left in little doubt that he had done that – I imagine, even better than his best expectations. So why would he come to me, knowing my reputation. I am not seeking to boast, Watson, but if Baroncourt had come to me, I could not see what more he hoped to obtain than he already had from Oldroyd and Hughes. It was a deal more likely that by retaining my services he risked my uncovering the whole of his ingenious plot.

"It took me some time to see the reason – I think, because it was audacious to a point of being almost unbelievable. The man who came to Baker Street was not Julius Baroncourt. It was Mr Smith!"

It *was* unbelievable! The risk of discovery must have been enormous – and I still didn't see the reason.

"There obviously was a risk," Holmes agreed, "but less than you might at first think. When Smith came here, he must have known that the murder of Silas Baroncourt was planned to take place less than two days later. He must equally have realised that he, Smith, was to be a second murder victim. That part of the plan he proposed to change. The second victim would be Julius Baroncourt and not he. He knew that once Julius Baroncourt was dead, the risk of my discovering the deception was greatly reduced.

"The 'reason' only becomes apparent when you put all of the pieces together. I was Mr Smith's insurance. He had clearly hoped that, after he had committed the murders, I would still wish to be involved. I, and perhaps you too, Watson, were two people who supposedly knew Julius Baroncourt and would be prepared to say that the man being questioned by the police at Selsdon was most certainly he. Strangely, Watson, you *have* seen the real Baroncourt, going into his club on the afternoon we were returning from Simpson's. But that is of little matter. I am telling you why I flatly refused to be involved in the police investigation of the two deaths. In the event, it made no difference. Smith's identity wasn't challenged – not surprisingly. No-one in Selsdon really knew Baroncourt, not even the railway porters, to whom he would have barely spoken. The occasion he had reported his double to the police was at 'A' Division in London, to a desk sergeant who could hardly be expected to remember the man's voice. The only danger to him were those people in London who did know Baroncourt quite well – like Lawrence Oldroyd. That was why he gave his evidence at the inquest in a whisper. His alleged 'illness' was no more than an excuse."

The Case of the Man who Followed Himself

I had no reason seriously to challenge anything that Holmes had said – though I did wonder about the true state of Smith's health. Certainly upon the occasion when I had last seen him, he appeared to be showing a quite abnormal degree of nervous agitation, which I could have thought genuine.

"I'm sure it was genuine!" was Holmes' response. "If you'd just been given a good reason for believing that a man whom you'd recently murdered had now returned to haunt you, *you* might well display such symptoms!"

....

Though the story so far, had not been without its surprises, I had succeeded in following it without too much difficulty. My success seemed, suddenly, at an end. I could recall nothing that had gone before which might even begin to explain Holmes' last remark.

"Nothing has gone before," he said, "and I had not intended to raise the point with so little finesse. I know that you don't understand, Watson. You will – and before you accuse me of it, I will plead guilty."

"To what?"

"'Using you', 'deceiving you', 'not showing my trust in you' – all of them accusations which you have levelled against me many times in the past, if not always with total justification. But I prevaricate. Very simply, my friend, nothing that I told you of what you assumed to be Baroncourt's unexpected appearance in Baker Street, my pursuing him to his club – and then his lodging, is true."

"But why the deception?" I asked.

"I will answer your question, Watson, but let me first remind you of something. The last time that we discussed this case at any length, I did say that there was nothing I had told you that I could prove. What I did not tell you at that time was that I believed the man living at Selsdon Park to be Mr Smith, and not Julius Baroncourt. I had not told it either to Macdonald, or Inspector Tripp – both of whom were quite convinced that it *was* Baroncourt.

"You, Watson, rightly suggested that if any progress were to be made, the only person who knew the truth was the man living at Selsdon Park, whoever he might be. I said that he might be persuaded.

"The means which I chose, you must already be beginning to see. I invented the appearances in Baker Street, at Boul's, and the lodging in the Edgware Road, and then wrote to Mr Smith, telling him about them. He had to respond as he did. Tripp has had him kept under discreet observation ever since the killings. Other than of necessity, he had never left the estate, much less been to London!"

"But Smith said he *had* been to London."

"Indeed he did. He'd had to invent a reason to invite us to the house. And that story had to

The Case of the Man who Followed Himself

explain his appearance in Baker Street, even though he knew he'd never been there. He was hardly going to tell us that he was being haunted, though he had to believe that he might be! That, Watson, was why I told you nothing. Your performance at Selsdon had to be totally convincing. There was no other way of ensuring it than by allowing you believe that it was the truth. I hope that you will regard it as the compliment intended, when I say that you are not an accomplished liar – I'd have to say – 'like myself'!"

It was a compliment, if compliment it truly was, which I could do no other than accept. Holmes continued.

"For the same reason, I had to keep you in ignorance even after our visit to Selsdon. Smith was going to check on what he could – the club, the lodging, the railway porter, even you, Watson. And he had to be given the right answers. He did telegraph his club, and he did speak to the railway porter. I knew that the man had to break. The only uncertainty was 'when'. That was why I had to utilise the services of the police – much as I would have preferred to work alone."

"But how did you know he would come to London?"

"Put yourself in his position Watson. He could see only two explanations of what had occurred. Either he was truly being haunted, or the man whom he believed he had murdered was not dead. He could, at least, attempt to establish the truth of the second of those alternatives. And where might he most likely begin?"

"At the lodgings of the man he believed he had murdered!"

"Precisely, Watson. And if he had been Baroncourt – as Macdonald and Tripp still believed, he would have taken us to Mr Smith's lodging, wherever that might be. But it was Baroncourt's lodging to which we were taken – that is why Macdonald remarked, 'It hasn't worked'."

It seemed that the explanation was almost at an end – but not yet. There remained what had stayed in my mind as the most mysterious and dramatic moments of the whole case – what happened in that third floor room from which Mr Smith had fallen to an untimely death.

"We shall never know for certain," Holmes said. "But there is a probable explanation. As you know, Watson, the post mortem has revealed a high alcohol content in the blood. Combined with a certain state of mind –"

"It's called 'mania-a-potu' – pathological intoxication. It produces an effect similar to that of certain narcotics, which might include hallucination."

"Thank you, Watson. You have answered your own question. If Smith was experiencing hallucinations, then what more likely than he 'saw' Baroncourt, the man he had murdered. He said, 'Why Baroncourt? I did no more to you than you had planned to do to me'. I imagine he threw

The Case of the Man who Followed Himself

something at what he believed he could see – so breaking the window. And then we must suppose that his vision advanced upon him, he backed away from it until he was pressed against the window. The already broken glass, and what later examination showed to be a rotten window frame, is enough to explain the rest."

"But, Holmes," I said. "I could have sworn that there were two people in that room. I distinctly saw two shadows on the curtains."

"Two gas lights in the room would cast two shadows. No, Watson. Smith was alone. He had locked himself in. There was no other way out – other than the way in which he did leave.

"You look unconvinced, my friend. Save it! Save it for the day when you might decide to commit this case to paper. It is an ending which would surely appeal to your sense of the dramatic. What I have told you, I am certain to be the truth. But you are entitled to an opinion, and who knows that you might not be right. Perhaps Mr Smith *was* literally frightened to death by the sight of his own waft!"